BERN DIBNER

C000119471

Oersted

and the Discovery of

ELECTROMAGNETISM

Blaisdell Publishing Company
NEW YORK   LONDON

SECOND EDITION

© Copyright, 1962, by Blaisdell Publishing Company

All rights reserved

Library of Congress Catalog Card Number: 63-14170

Manufactured in the United States of America

. . .　　　Call Pythagoras and bid
The sage to mark the laws divine which rule
Each planet's course, and when he reads and sees
such harmony amidst the countless worlds,
Trembling with joy his heart will overflow
Before the sacred concert of high reason.

—OERSTED, *The Soul in Nature*

Acknowledgements

Thanks are herewith extended to those who have helped in the preparation of this monograph. Especially included are the typist and artist. Special thanks are due to the friends in Denmark whose generosity in sharing portraits, photos, books, and other information is gratefully acknowledged.

Contents

Voltaic Electricity Announced

A new epoch commenced in 1800 when Alessandro Volta announced his discovery of a way of producing continuous-current electricity. On March 20, of that year, a letter was dispatched by Volta from his home in Como, Italy, to Sir Joseph Banks, President of the Royal Society in London. Because a state of war existed between England and France, the letter arrived in two sections and was finally read before the Royal Society on June 26, 1800. It was subsequently published in the *Transactions of the Royal Society* that year. No other event was more influential in shaping modern history.

At that time, the air in the nations on both sides of the Atlantic was charged with revolutionary zeal and promise. The young United States had not yet attained its majority as a nation; indeed its first president had died but a few months before. France was gripped by revolutionary excitement in which Reason had replaced Faith, new ideas in society were being instituted, and science was given a new and prominent place in the revolutionary program. Luigi Galvani's announcement in 1791 of his discovery and demonstration of "animal electricity" had revealed the presence of forces in nature that had previously been unknown. The growth in number and influence of experimental societies and the correspondence between amateurs of experiment had stimulated the search for more of the unknown forces and newly disclosed relationships in the physical and biological world. Galvani had influenced Volta into repeating experiments to demonstrate the presence of animal electricity. Although first in agreement with Galvani's interpretation, Volta, a keen and exhaustive experimenter, reached a different conclusion as to the causes of the muscular action wherein excised animal tissue, such as dissected frogs' legs, would go into convulsive motion when touched by joined prods of dissimilar metals.

Thus, events in the laboratories led to the development of the Voltaic pile and an entirely new form of electrical excitation was made possible. An electric *current* flowed in a circuit formed by a wire connecting pairs of disks or strips of dissimilar metals immersed in brine or a weak acid electrolyte.

The first of two forms of electrical device featured in Volta's communication to the Royal Society consisted of a pile of silver and zinc disks, each pair of which was separated from the adjoining pairs by paper or cloth separators soaked in brine. The second form that Volta developed to illustrate a variant source of constant-flow electricity was his "crown of cups." This consisted of a ring of cups filled with brine and connected by alternate strips of zinc and silver joined by metallic jumpers. This was an improvement over the pile because it avoided the weakening of the current flow as the brine in the separators dried.

Further improvements occurred when copper replaced silver and when dilute sulphuric acid was substituted for brine in the cups. With these piles, wires connecting the two outer elements were shown to be capable of decomposing water, melting fine filaments of metal, stimulating muscular contraction in animals and creating a sour taste upon the tongue.

So startling was the announcement of Volta's discovery that scientists on both sides of the Atlantic repeated and expanded Volta's experiments. In November 1801, Volta demonstrated the action of the new electrical source in Paris before an assembly of scientists attended also by the First Consul, Napoleon Bonaparte, in a session that brought the

Sculpture after Berra; Burndy Library

ALESSANDRO VOLTA

Stimulated by the work of Galvani in "animal electricity," Volta, professor of physics at Pavia, discovered a chemical source of constant-current electricity with the invention of the voltaic pile. This opened a new era in science.

[3]

two men into conversation for several hours. Napoleon proposed to his minister, Chaptal, that prizes be established to encourage new research into galvanism, adding, "Galvanism, in my opinion, will lead to great discoveries."* One prize was to be awarded to the one who contributed experiments or discoveries in electricity or magnetism comparable to those given to these sciences by Benjamin Franklin and Volta.

The stage was set for yet another step in scientific evolution. On a cosmic scale we have, in the history of science, examples of the development of theories that depended on the slow accumulation of data from which, by analysis and induction, a Copernicus proposed the heliocentric system or a Darwin, the doctrine of evolution. In the case history we are now examining, the discovery of electromagnetism is an instance of a simple but prime relationship between basic physical forces that eluded recognition and formulation for two active decades in spite of the many minds that were concerned with related phenomena.

The Electrochemists

Even before the delayed second part of Volta's letter had reached the Royal Society, the chemist William Nicholson, aided by the English surgeon Anthony Carlisle, constructed a voltaic pile and proceeded with chemical experiments. Water was decomposed by the pile, which consisted of seventeen large silver coins separated by an equal number

* Fahie, J. J, *History of the Electric Telegraph,* London, 1884, p. 270. A full reference Bibliography will be found on page 77.

of copper disks. Each such pair was separated from the adjoining pairs by bits of cloth soaked in a weak brine solution. Gas was observed to bubble at the juncture of the conducting wire to the pile, where a drop of water had been added to improve the conductivity of the juncture. This crude assembly was replaced on May 2, 1800, by a glass tube filled with water and having brass wires connected to the pile terminals entering each end of the tube through a cork

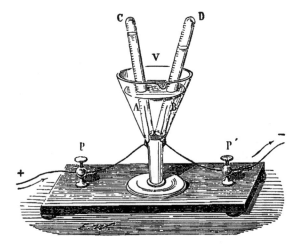

FIGUIER, *p 630*

The earliest application of Volta's newly discovered source of constant-current electricity was in the decomposition of water by Nicholson and Carlisle in England and by Ritter in Germany.

stopper. Hydrogen formed at the negative terminal and oxygen at the positive one. William Cruickshank repeated and confirmed the experiments of Nicholson and Carlisle showing that hydrogen evolved from the silver or copper section of the pile and oxygen from the zinc. When litmus coloring was added to the water, the zinc end showed a red tinge in the fluid near the terminal. This phenomenon was seized upon by several inventors as a means for distant electric telegraphy. Cruickshank also improved the voltaic pile by arranging rectangular zinc and copper plates in a resin-insulated wooden trough and with this decomposed several compounds and electroplated metals.

A new research tool came into the hands of the experimenter. The spectacular experiments performed in the late 1700's with the use of electrostatic generators gave way to experiments using the more prosaic and corrosive electric battery. Sparks, halos, and pinwheels were replaced by the deeper and more challenging phenomena that issued from the ends of an electric battery assembly.

In England, the most ambitious experimenter with the new source of electricity was Humphry Davy, professor of chemistry at the Royal Institution in London. With the help of William H. Pepys, an instrument maker and Fellow of the Royal Society, the strongest voltaic pile of its time was constructed in February 1802 for Davy. It consisted of sixty pairs of zinc and copper plates, each 6 inches square. With this, Davy melted iron wires up to 1/10 inch in diameter and platinum wires 1/32 inch in diameter. Gold, silver, and lead sheets were made to glow and ignite. Using an even more powerful battery of 274 plates which Pepys had constructed, Davy, in October 1807, was able to decompose alkalis, obtaining potash and soda ash from which he extracted the new elements potassium and sodium. In the following year, 1808, a battery of 2000 pairs of plates of zinc and copper was constructed at the Royal Institution by Pepys and with this Davy drew his most brilliant electric arc and extracted additional new elements—barium, strontium, calcium, and magnesium—from alkaline earths. He ignited cotton, sulphur, resin, and ether. Iron, quartz, sapphire, and platinum were melted, diamond evaporated, and liquids such as water and oil were boiled by the electric current. The intense heat developed by this battery was used by Pepys in 1815 to melt a short section of iron wire and diamond dust together, thereby directly carburizing the iron and making steel.

Also associated with Davy was William H. Wollaston, a physician who abandoned the practice of medicine for the scientific investigations that intrigued him. He experimented widely with voltaic electricity and among the thirty-eight papers he contributed to the Royal Society were those proposing the theory that the oxidation of metals was the primary cause of the generation of an electric current in a voltaic pile. He examined spectra of the electric arc as early as 1802 and improved the form of the electric battery, exposing both sides of a zinc plate by placing the plate within the separated but adjacent faces of a bent U-shaped copper plate.

In 1813, although England and France were at war, Davy traveled on the Continent with his assistant, Michael Faraday, discussing his work in Paris with Humboldt, Gay-Lussac, Count Rumford, and Ampère. He also visited several scientists in Switzerland and Volta in Italy.

To enlarge the area of electrical investigation, a very large and effective battery was constructed by John G. Children in 1809; it consisted of twenty pairs of copper and zinc plates, each plate 6 feet long and 2 feet 8 inches wide. Children confirmed observations, made by Davy and also by Professor Robert Hare of the University of Pennsylvania, that the *intensity* of the electric current increased with the number of plates whereas the *quantity* of electric flow depended on the extent of the plate surface. With this battery Children rendered a bar of platinum, $\frac{1}{6}$ inch square and 2 and $\frac{1}{4}$ inches long, red-hot by the current. He also arranged an order of relative conductivity of metals, concluding that silver conducted the current best, then zinc, gold, copper, iron, and platinum, of least conductivity. Tin and lead were fused immediately by the current. Children, like Davy, applied current to a circuit, cutting a slot across an iron wire which he then filled with diamond powder. On the passing of the electric current through the circuit, the diamond liquefied and the contiguous iron turned to steel.

An air of contentment with the record of discovery spread in England. In 1818, Bostock wrote, "It may be conjectured that we have carried the power of the instrument to the utmost extent of which it admits; and it does not appear that we are at present in the way of making any important additions to our knowledge of its effects, or of obtaining any new light upon the theory of its action."*

In Italy one of the most active experimenters with the pile was the former pupil and colleague of Volta, the mineralogist Luigi G. Brugnatelli. He investigated the processes of plating by electricity and managed to coat two large silver medals which had been immersed in a saturated solution of chloride of gold treated by ammonia, and succeeded in covering them with a plate of gold.

Credit for the clearest exposition of the chemical nature of the voltaic battery has been given to George F. Parrot, a Russian physician and a professor of chemistry at the University of Dorpat, in Estonia, whose many papers appeared in German in Gilbert's *Annalen der Physik* in 1802, 1805, 1817, and 1819.

In France, in 1808, Gay-Lussac and Thénard were provided with a battery of 600 pairs of plates which Napoleon had presented to the École Polytechnique and which was

---

* Bostock, John, *Account of the History and Present State of Galvanism,* London, 1818, p 102. The "instrument" he referred to was the voltaic pile

[8]

built on the pattern suggested by Cruickshank. With this battery of 1800 square feet of metallic surface, chemical decomposition was investigated, especially that of alkalis, and reported in a work of two volumes,* published in Paris in 1811.

Germany, too. had its share of investigators into the action of voltaic electricity. An important contribution was made by Johann W. Ritter (1776-1810). He was the first to observe and publish, in Jena in 1800, on the electrolytic decomposition of water, and he devised the first storageable pile, which became known as a "charging" or "secondary" pile. This consisted of disks of a single metal separated by circular pieces of cloth or cardboard wetted by a liquid that would not affect the metal. Ritter showed that if this new pile were placed within the terminals of a voltaic pile, a portion of the electric charge would be retained and the Ritter pile would act as a source of electric current which, like the original source, would produce electric sparks, give shocks and decompose water. Ritter was also reported to have electrically charged a gold needle pivoted on its center and to have observed that the needle assumed a position of dip or deflection which remained constant after each charge. However, the angle differed from that of a magnetic needle, which assumed the usual angle of dip. Ritter's experiments, like those of many other investigators of the period, seemed too uncertain or inconsistent in behavior when repeated by other experimenters and too broad in the conclusions drawn from them. They therefore received little attention in the scientific press of the time.

Another area of investigation of the performance of voltaic electricity was the distances over which the current could be made to travel. Friedrich H. Basse of the romantic

---

* Entitled, *Recherches Physico-chymiques faites sur la Pile*

town of Hameln in Hannover transmitted an electric current over 500 feet of wire suspended on fir posts along the frozen water of the moat surrounding the town. In the circuit were a voltaic battery and an electroscope which registered the circulating current. Later experiments were made across a meadow some 3500 feet long, using the ground as the return section of the circuit.

Shortly after several experimenters first constructed voltaic piles, an effort was made to determine the speed of electricity in traversing an electrical conductor. Giovanni Aldini, a nephew of Galvani and an author of considerable prominence, reported his own experiments in 1804 in his two-volume *Essai* (also the source of an electromagnetic controversy). He extended a wire between Fort-Rouge and the west jetty in the harbor of Calais. Using a voltaic pile of eighty plates of silver and zinc, he completed the circuit from the pile to an overhead wire, then into a small chamber holding a dissected animal to register the electric shock when the circuit was completed. Another wire then led down into the harbor, the water carrying the current the 15 meters across to the lower terminal of the pile. His conclusion was that the current traveled with "astonishing rapidity."

To foster experimentation in voltaic currents, a society was formed in Paris called the French Galvanic Society. This group published accounts of its experiments and maintained correspondence in countries outside of France. In 1815 the Magnetic Society was founded in Paris, but it lasted only five years and was concerned primarily with "animal magnetism" and the medical and psychological aspects of mesmerism.

On the American side, Robert Hare, Professor of Chemistry at the University of Pennsylvania, published an account

Legend del.

Blanchard Sculp.

ALDINI, plate 8

An experiment in 1803 by Aldini to determine the speed of electric flow along a wire stretched across the bay at Calais. The indicator of circuit completion was by shock to a human, or muscular contraction in a dissected animal. Although a wire return in the water is indicated, none was used.

FIGUIER, p. 669

The powerful voltaic battery constructed at the Polytechnic Institute in Paris in 1813 by order of Napoleon who showed exceptional interest in the development of electricity.

[12]

of a new battery constructed in Philadelphia. Basically, this consisted of long sheets of zinc and copper contiguously rolled into coils, but kept ½ inch apart. Eighty such coils were suspended by a frame which was lowered into and raised from glass vessels containing an acid solution. Investigations by Professor Hare with this apparatus led him to the concept of *quantity* and *intensity* of the resultant electric current, depending on the number and size of the exposed plates, respectively. He thus joined Green and Hazard, other Philadelphia experimenters, in an effort to determine the chemical nature of the voltaic pile. Professor J. R. Coxe, also a Philadelphia chemist, had proposed an electrochemical telegraph, based on the decomposition of water.

The electrochemical experiments of Davy, the Swedish chemist Berzelius, and other chemists led to the discovery of new earth metals, to the plating of metals by electricity, and to the brilliance of the arc light; but these were not the only practical results of Volta's great contribution. Two additional practical uses were found for the electric current— exploding gunpowder at a distance by an electric fuse and telegraphy, also at a distance, by the use of electric currents. Charles W. Pasley, an officer in the British Army, followed a suggestion by Mr. W. Palmer who proposed the use of a voltaic battery to ignite gunpowder by creating a spark, instead of the long powder fuse which was then commonly used. Later, in 1812, Baron Paul L. Schilling, attaché to the Russian Embassy in Munich, insulated a copper wire and a thin coat of india rubber and varnish, and stretched this wire under ground and under water so as to explode powder mines across the river Neva near St. Petersburg. This was also done across the Seine during the occupation of Paris by the allied armies following the collapse of Napoleon. The demonstration of exploding gunpowder across the Seine was an astonishing sight to those who first witnessed it but did not understand the technique used.

The application of the voltaic battery as a source of energy to operate an electrochemical telegraph was tried many times during the period 1800 to 1820, but with indifferent results. The outstanding effort was the apparatus developed by Samuel T. von Soemmering, German physician, whose equipment created a considerable stir in scientific circles. In 1809, at the Academy of Science in Munich, he successfully demonstrated the telegraph over a distance of 1000 feet. It consisted of thirty-five gold rods set into glass tubes placed at the bottom of a tank having glass walls and partially filled with acidulated water. To these rods were connected thirty-five wires wrapped in silk. The wires led from a wooden stand having thirty-five copper apertures connected to one terminal of a voltaic pile. When the other terminal was touched to the wire ends of the thirty-five leads (representing twenty-five letters and ten figures) gas bubbles would rise in the distant tank and would so indicate which letter or figure was being transmitted. Albeit slow and clumsy, still this was a working mechanism and was greatly admired. General Larrey, Napoleon's chief surgeon, carried Soemmering's telegraph to the French Academy of Sciences where a committee of outstanding physicists studied and rendered a report on its operation. In the two subsequent years, von Soemmering reduced the number of wires required for the telegraph to twenty-seven and in 1812 the distance of its operation was extended to nearly 2 miles.

Further improvements in this form of electric telegraph were suggested in 1811 by Johann S. C. Schweigger (1779-1857), a chemist of Halle, Germany, who recommended the reduction of the many wires to simply two conductors by the use of two voltaic batteries of unequal power. The combination of these three elements could, Schweigger held, provide the needed combinations to transmit all the letters and figures, if longer and shorter periods of gas generation were to be employed. He also recommended the use of a pistol triggered by the battery to signal the beginning of a message, instead of indications by accumulated gas, such as Soemmering used.*

The search for a relationship between voltaic electricity (referred to in that period as "galvanism") and magnetism was investigated by many competent experimenters during the period 1800 to 1820. Especially noteworthy were the investigations made in 1805 by Hachette and Desormes. They constructed a battery of 1480 thin copper plates coated with zinc, and this pile was set on a float resting on the water in a large vat. No orientation with the earth's magnetic field was observed, although a steel bar magnet which weighed nearly half as much as the pile itself, and was floated in the same way, moved in a series of oscillations until it rested in the magnetic meridian.† It was noted that the poles of the pile were not joined during the experiment. Another effort to link electricity to magnetism was made by Johann P. Prechtl of Trieste and the Vienna Polytechnic Institute in 1810. However it was found that his exposition of diagrams and mode of reasoning proved too complex to impress his readers.

---

* Soemmering's apparatus was described and illustrated in the *Denkschriften der Konigl Akademie der Wissenschaften,* Muenchen, 1809-1810, issued in 1811, pp 401-414.

† Described in Mottelay, P. F., *Biographical History of Electricity and Magnetism,* London, 1922, p. 376.

The Elusive Force

A review of the 20 years* following the discovery of voltaic electricity clearly shows a continued and intense interest in almost every phase of investigation made possible by the introduction of a source of constant-current electricity. The chemists were exceptionally busy theorizing and experimenting to determine the physics and chemistry of electric generation. Although many corollary effects and physical manifestations of the electrical and electrochemical experiments were investigated, what seems to us now as a most obvious relationship—the magnetic effects of an electric current—seems to have been missed. When we hunt for the clear and specific observation (inevitably to be made by some keen investigator), it may seem incredible that it should have required 20 years of experimenting and observing finally to present that fact in complete clarity. Thus we see that Nicholas Gautherot (1753-1803) a French chemist, had observed as early as 1801, that two wires, one connected to one end of an electric battery and the other to the other end, would tend to adhere to one another when these two wires were brought in close contact.† Not only was this

---

* In the period between 1800 and 1820, representing the time between the discovery of voltaic electricity and Oersted's discovery of electromagnetism, the Wheeler Gift catalog of early electrical publications lists 68 books, pamphlets and notices published in nine countries that were concerned with constant-flow electrical experiments, an indication of the wide order of interest and experimentation being then carried out. This work catalogs the collection formed by the English telegraph pioneer Latimer Clark (1822-1898), bought by Schuyler S. Wheeler and presented to the American Institute of Electrical Engineers in 1901. It lists 7000 titles and was published in two volumes, New York, 1909, with notes by W. D Weaver and M F O'Reilly.

† Reported in *Annales de Chimie,* Volume 39, p 209

observation repeated in 1806 by such experimenters as C. J. Lehot, a French physicist, but the phenomenon was independently observed by both Laplace and Biot.

Gian Domenico Romagnosi,* in 1802, Benedetto Mojon, in 1804, and others reported experiments even less specific in associating magnetism with electricity. These reports had negligible effect on the many investigators. The impact of Oersted's great discovery and announcement is in sharp contrast with the uncertain trials, hints, and suggestions of the earlier experimenters.

On July 21, 1820 there appeared a four-page notice in Copenhagen, in Latin, announcing Oersted's discovery of electromagnetism. This literally electrified the entire scientific world. As rapidly as word could be gotten from mouth to ear, by traveler or visitor, in private conversation or in the lecture hall, the substance of Oersted's short announcement was spread. The physical world and man's institutions could never again be the same, now that Oersted presented the first rich fruit of Volta's epochal discovery.

Hans Christian Oersted

The boyhood of Oersted represented a minimal chance of either attaining greatness or serving his people so well and over so long a span of life. He was born in the small Danish town of Rudkoebing on the island of Langeland in the south-central part of Denmark on August 14, 1777. His father, Soeren, was the village apothecary whose slender in-

---

* His experiment is further described on page 43.

come made it difficult to feed his family, let alone educate them in a town without even a school. The two older boys, Hans and Anders, his junior by a year, therefore went daily to the home of Oldenburg, a warm and friendly wigmaker nearby, for instruction in German; his wife taught the two boys to read and write Danish. Other brothers later joined them for instruction with Oldenburg, the wigmaker, and also arithmetic was added to Bible reading, German, and Danish in the informal curriculum. Oldenburg's contributions were soon exhausted and the boys had to turn to a wider circle of the town's learned, including the pastor, to supplement the simple teaching. From the town surveyor Hans learned drawing and mathematics; from a university student, some academic subjects. The mayor of the town taught them English and French. Whatever Hans or Anders learned separately, each passed on to the other; they read every book that they could borrow in the village. At twelve, Hans was sufficiently mature to help his father in the apothecary shop; this helped stimulate his interest in medicine and science. His earlier love for literature and history remained with him for his entire life.

In 1793 the brothers decided to enter the University of Copenhagen (founded in 1479) and the following spring found them at the university preparing to matriculate for the autumn session. While Hans devoted himself to the sciences of medicine, physics, and astronomy, Anders studied law.* The brothers continued to help each other during

---

* Anders Sandoe Oersted later became the foremost jurist in Denmark and a Minister of State. He married the sister of Adam G. Oehlenschlaeger, a fellow student at the university, who rose to become Denmark's foremost literary figure and remained Hans' best friend for his entire life. Oehlenschlaeger described the student days of the Oersteds as secluded, "walking arm in arm in long yellow greatcoats. . . . They sat here, grave, silent, at their studies, as in a dim monastic cell."

their studies, sharing a joint purse, lodging together in the dormitory, and dining together at the home of their aunt. They supplemented their income by small government assistance, by tutoring, and by economizing wherever they could. So impressive were those serious years of study at the university that Hans later wrote, "to be perfectly free, the young man must revel in the great kingdom of thought and imagination; there is a struggle there, in which, if he falls, it is easy for him to rise again, there is freedom of utterance there, which draws after it no irreparable consequences on society. . . . I lived in this onward-driving contest where each day overcame a new difficulty, gained a new truth, or banished a previous error."* He openly proclaimed his pleasure in lecturing and writing about science. In 1797, his third year at the university, Hans was awarded the first important token of recognition, a gold medal for his essay on "Limits of Poetry and Prose." He completed his training in pharmacy also, taking his degree with high honors in 1797.† In 1799 he was awarded the degree of Doctor of Philosophy along with a prize for an essay in medicine. He proposed a fresh theory of alkalis which later was accepted in chemical practices.

Hans' student days were at a time when Europe was in a new intellectual ferment following the revolutions in America and in France. Germany and Italy were rising from

---

* Quoted in Munro, John, *Pioneers of Electricity*, London, 1890, p 145

† De Beaumont, in his *Éloge historique de Oersted*, Paris, 1862, p 6, referred to the examination of Oersted in pharmacy and stated how he astonished his examiners by the extent of his knowledge. One of the examiners remarked to Professor Manthey, "What a candidate you have sent us, he knows more about it than all of us do."

divisive nationalisms and a strong wave of intellectual aware-
ness was sweeping the Continent.

The new century opened with Oersted beginning his
professional career in charge of an apothecary shop in
Copenhagen and as lecturer at the university. He was stirred
by the announcement of Volta's discovery of chemical electricity and he immediately applied the voltaic pile to experiments with acids and alkalis. The following year he devoted
to the customary *Wanderjahr,* traveling in Germany, France,
and the Netherlands, meeting the philosophers Schelling,
Fichte, and Tieck. He also met Count Rumford (born
Benjamin Thompson in Woburn, Massachusetts) who was
then serving the Elector of Bavaria, and the physicist Ritter;
these were Oersted's main contacts in science.

From Göttingen (1801), where he stayed for ten days,
he wrote, "The first question asked everywhere is about
galvanism. As everybody is curious to see the battery of glass
tubes I have invented, I have had quite a small one made
here of four glass tubes (in Copenhagen I used thirty) and
intend to carry it with me."* Oersted joined Ritter at Jena
and stayed with him for three weeks, continuing their correspondence after he left. With Ritter he was exposed to
the fantastic profusion of ideas that stormed through his
host's fertile but disorganized mind. Oersted remodeled
Ritter's notes into an essay in French which was submitted
to the Institut de France for its annual prize of 3000 francs
The sound discoveries of this quixotic genius were so diluted
by those of fantasy that the prize was never awarded to him.
In May 1803, Ritter, in another flight of fancy, wrote to
Oersted a letter that contained a remarkable prophecy. He
related events on earth to periodic celestial phenomena and

---

* Meyer, Kirstine, *H. C Oersted, Scientific Papers,* Copenhagen,
1920, Vol. I, p. XXIV.

indicated that the years of maximum inclination of the ecliptic coincided with the years of important electrical discoveries. Thus, 1745 corresponded to the invention of the "Leiden" jar by Kleist; 1764 that of the electrophorus by Wilcke; 1782 produced the condenser of Volta; and 1801 the voltaic pile. Ritter proceeded, "You now emerge into a new epoch in which late in the year 1819 or 1820, you will have to reckon. This we might well witness."* Ritter died in 1810 and Oersted not only lived to see the event occur, but was the author of it.

In 1803 Oersted returned to Copenhagen and applied for the university's chair in physics but was rejected because he was probably considered more a philosopher than a physicist. He continued experimenting and lecturing, publishing the results of his experiments in German and Danish periodicals. In 1806 his ambition was realized and he became Professor of Physics at the Copenhagen University, although not realizing full professorship (ordinarius) until 1817.†

During Oersted's attendance at the university, it was poorly equipped with physical apparatus for experimenting in the sciences. He was, however, fortunate in his contact with Professor J. G. L. Manthey (1769-1842), teacher of chemistry, who, in addition to his academic chair, was also proprietor of the Lion Pharmacy in Copenhagen where Oersted assisted him. Manthey maintained a valuable collection of physical and chemical apparatus which was at Oersted's disposal during his student days and after his

---

* Meyer, Vol. I, p XXXIII.

† The academic awards granted by the university to Oersted may be summed up as Doctor of Philosophy in 1799, Adjunct in 1800, Professor extraordinarius in 1806 and Professor ordinarius in 1817. The status of "ordinarius" was higher than that of "extraordinarius."

graduation. In 1800, Manthey went abroad and Oersted was appointed manager of the Lion Pharmacy. In February 1801, Oersted did manage to experiment with physical apparatus and reported experiments made with a voltaic battery of 600 plates of zinc and silver and later experiments with a battery of sixty plates of zinc and lead. In 1803, Oersted, simultaneously with Davy, discovered that acids increased the strength of a voltaic battery more than did salts. Eager as he was to pursue this promising line, he was so loaded down with the management of the pharmacy and lectures in the medical and pharmaceutical faculties at the university that he could devote only Sunday afternoons to "galvanizing."

He assumed his academic career with the same intensity and thoroughness that had marked every step in his rise from boyhood. The university was the only one in Denmark and the status of professor represented the upper social level. His broad interest in literary, political, and philosophical movements opened many doors to him. His friends were numerous and their ties to him were strong.

The years 1812 and 1813 saw him in Germany and France again, but on this visit to Berlin he did not seek out the philosophers as he had on his first journey. In Berlin, he published in German his views of the chemical laws of nature; this was issued in French translation (Paris, 1813) under the title *Recherches sur l'identité des forces chimiques et électriques,* a work held in very high esteem by the new generation of research chemists. His interest in finding a relationship between voltaic electricity and magnetism is here first indicated. Chapter VIII is entitled On Magnetism and in it are included such remarks as, "One has always been tempted to compare the magnetic forces with the electrical forces. The great resemblance between electrical and magnetic attractions and repulsions and the similarity of their laws necessarily would bring about this comparison. It is true, that nothing has been found comparable with electricity by communication; but the phenomena observed had such a degree of analogy to those depending on electrical distribution that one could not find the slightest difference. . . . The form of galvanic activity is halfway between the magnetic form and the electrical form. There, forces are more latent than in electricity, and less than in magnetism. . . . But in such an important question, we would be satisfied if the judgment were that the principal objection to the identity of forces which produce electricity and magnetism were only a difficulty, and not a thing which is contrary to it. . . . One could also add to these analogies that steel loses its magnetism by heat, which proves that steel becomes a better conductor through a rise in temperature, just as electrical bodies do. It is also found that magnetism exists in all bodies of nature, as proven by Bruckmann and Coulomb. By that, one feels that magnetic forces are as general as electrical forces. An attempt should be made to see if electricity, in its most latent stage, has any action on the magnet as such." His plan and intent were clearly charted.

Oersted returned in 1814 and resumed an active part in university and political discussions. In one debate, he supported the freedom of judgment as opposed to dogma; in another, he held that the practice of science was, in fact, an act of religious worship. He continued as a popular lecturer. He devised a detonating fuse in which a short wire was caused to glow by an electric current. In 1819, under royal command, he undertook a very successful geological expedition to Bornholm, one of the Danish islands, being one of three scientists in the expedition. It was with the assistance of one of the members of this expedition, Lauritz Esmarch, that Oersted succeeded in producing light by creating an electric discharge in mercury vapor through which an electric current was made to flow. Together they also developed a new form of voltaic cell in which the wooden trough was replaced by one of copper, thereby producing stronger currents. Esmarch was among those who witnessed Oersted's first demonstration of his discovery.

Discovery of Electromagnetism

The association between electrical (both electrostatic and voltaic) forces and magnetic forces had been recognized by investigators for many decades. Electrical literature contained numerous references to lightning that had magnetized iron and had altered the polarity of compass needles. In the late 1700's Beccaria and van Marum, among others, had magnetized iron by sending electrostatic charge through it. Beccaria had almost stumbled on a lead to the relationship between electricity and magnetism when a discharge from a Leyden jar was sent *transversally* through a piece of watch-spring steel making its ends magnetic. The resulting magnetic effect proved to be stronger than the effect of a discharge made lengthwise. Although the experiments of Romagnosi and others, cited above, had already been noted, no one had determined the cause-and-effect relationship between the electric and magnetic forces.* Oersted's own earlier experiments were unimpressive, possibly because he

---

* The subject of the relationships of electricity and magnetism is further treated on page 42

had, like other experimenters, laid the conducting wire across the compass needle instead of parallel with it.

The sequence of events leading to his important discovery still remains ambiguous but it seems that one of the advanced students at the university related that the first

FIGUIER, p. 713

Lecturing before a select group of students, Oersted, in the spring of 1820, noticed that the needle of a nearby magnetic compass deviated when the circuit of a voltaic pile was completed. On July 21 the discovery of electromagnetism was announced.

direct event that led to the publication of Oersted's discovery occurred during a private lecture made before a group of other advanced students in the spring of 1820. At this lecture Oersted happened to place a conducting wire over and parallel with a magnetic needle. Another student related that the experiment concerned the heating of some platinum wire by means of an electric current and that a compass needle happened by chance to be near and underneath the conducting wire. In any case, Oersted observed the needle to swing strongly aside as though a magnet had been moved close to it. Not much was said or done at the moment, but the challenging problem had fixed itself in Oersted's mind, and later, using a more powerful battery and larger conductor, he repeated the experiment with startling results. He then organized the problem, formulated the observations and arrived at a set of conclusions which he prepared into one of the most famous and rare bits of scientific literature.* This four-page tract appeared on July 21, 1820 in Latin, bearing the title *Experimenta circa effectum conflictus electrici in acum magneticam.*† It announced that an electric current in a conductor creates a circular magnetic field around the conductor. Further, if a magnetic needle is brought into the field surrounding the wire, it will set itself tangent to the circular field, continuing its tangential position if the needle is carried around the wire, pointing in one

---

* Only two (or at most, three) copies of this rare tract are known to exist in America in the original form in which it was privately printed and circulated by Oersted to friends and science groups in Europe. One of these ephemera is in the Burndy Library, another in the famous collection of scientific discoveries gathered by Dr. Herbert McLean Evans of Berkeley, California

† *Experiments on the Effects of a Current of Electricity (or Electrical Conflict) on the Magnetic Needle.* A translation of this announcement into English appears in the Appendix

direction beneath the wire and in the opposite direction when above it. If the direction of current is reversed in the conductor, the direction of the needle is similarly reversed from its former position. Various substances interposed between wire and needle had no effect on the position of the latter. Incredibly simple as this relationship seems to be, it remained unobserved during two decades of investigation by many penetrating minds.*

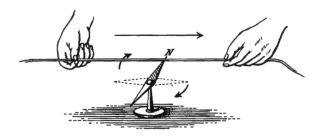

In essence, Oersted's discovery was that a wire carrying an electric current affected an adjacent magnetic needle by causing it to swerve to a position perpendicular to the direction of the wire When the current was reversed, the needle swung diametrically about When the wire was placed under the needle, it pointed in the opposite direction, indicating a magnetic field circular in form around the conductor

Oersted's failure to publish a detailed account of how he came upon his discovery, of exactly what the series of confirming experiments consisted, or the time and place of each step in the process of clarification have left an area of uncertainty that never has quite been filled. Five general

---

* The 20-year period between the discovery of the pile by Volta and that of electromagnetism by Oersted, as treated by Mottelay in his *Bibliographical History of Electricity and Magnetism*, covers 118 pages of description of the electrical events, announcements and discoveries, mostly with voltaic current, that occurred during those years

accounts have been left to us by Oersted concerning events connected with the discovery. The earliest of these was published in Danish before April 1821* and was immediately followed by two equivalent accounts in German and French† also probably prepared by Oersted. In these accounts Oersted stated, "I was brought back to them (experiments on the effects of an electric current on a magnet) through my lectures on electricity, galvanism, and magnetism in the spring of 1820. The auditors were mostly men already considerably advanced in science; so these lectures and the preparatory reflections led me on to deeper investigations than those which are admissible in ordinary lectures. Thus my former conviction of the identity of electrical and magnetic forces developed with new clarity, and I resolved to test my opinion by experiment. The preparations for this were made on a day in which I had to give a lecture on the same evening. I there showed Canton's experiment on the influence of chemical effects on the magnetic state of iron. I called attention to the variations of the magnetic needle during a thunderstorm, and at the same time I set forth the conjecture that an electric discharge could act on a magnetic needle placed outside the galvanic circuit. I then resolved to make the experiment. Since I expected the greatest effect

---

* This account appeared in the *Review of the Royal Danish Society of Sciences* for May 1820–May 1821; Oersted was the society's secretary. The text was reprinted in Meyer, Vol. II, pp 447-453.

† Schweigger's *Journal für Chemie und Physik*, 1821, vol. 32, pp. 199-231. A French version appeared in the *Journal de Physique*, 1821, vol 93, pp. 161-180. A comparison between the German and French versions was made by Prof. Robert C. Stauffer and published in ISIS, March 1957, p. 45; he provided a fresh translation from which the extract quoted here was copied

from a discharge associated with incandescence, I inserted in the circuit a very fine platinum wire above the place where the needle was located. The effect was certainly unmistakable, but still it seemed to me so confused that I postponed further investigation to a time when I hoped to have more leisure.* At the beginning of July these experiments were resumed and continued without interruption until I arrived at the results which have been published.

* All my auditors are witnesses that I mentioned the result of the experiment beforehand. The discovery was therefore not made by accident, as Professor Gilbert has wished to conclude from the expressions I used in my first announcement "

The two later accounts of the genesis of his discovery were written in 1827. One was in autobiographical form. Looking back on the seven years since the announcement of his discovery, Oersted referred to his epochal paper, "This half-sheet was now sent on the same post day to the most important scientific centers in Europe. The experiments were soon repeated in all countries in which there were friends of science and the greatest reward an inventor can enjoy, that of seeing his invention become the object of the most industrious investigation, seeing it expanded and fructifying, was his to the fullest. The number of those who have written on electromagnetism amounts to well over a hundred. Therefore, with the united efforts of so many, this knowledge too has been expanded and enriched in content far beyond what one would expect in the short period of seven years."†

---

† Published in Hans A Kofod's *Conversations-Lexicon*, XXVIII, Copenhagen, 1828, pp. 536-8.

The fifth account Oersted prepared in English for the *Edinburgh Encyclopedia,* 1830* and it appeared as an article entitled "Thermo-Electricity." Using the third person, Oersted reviewed the history of magnetic effects resulting from electrical charges, including the investigations of Franklin, Wilcke, and van Marum. He then referred to the report on Mojon's experiment "that a steel needle having been 22 days in communication with a galvanical apparatus of 100 elements, had become magnetical—an experiment which would have been of no historical interest if its author had not founded upon it, 18 years later, a pretension to the discovery of electromagnetism." He then referred the mention of Romagnosi made by Giovanni Aldini in his *Essai,* and added, "It is, therefore, not surprising that neither the French institute, nor the other learned societies, nor the numerous natural philosophers, to which the work was presented in the year 1804, took any notice of this observation, which would have accelerated the discovery of electromagnetism by sixteen years. Romanesi seems likewise to have forgot his observation, until electromagnetism was discovered." He then stated that "Electromagnetism itself, was discovered in the year 1820, by Professor Hans Christian Oersted, of the University of Copenhagen. Throughout his literary career, he adhered to the opinion, that the magnetical effects are produced by the same powers as the electrical. . . . In a treatise . . . translated into French, 1813, he endeavoured to establish a general chemical theory, in harmony with this principle. In this work, he proved that not only chemical affinities, but also heat and light are produced by the same two powers, which probably might be only two

* On pp. 573-89. The editor was David Brewster. The report is repeated in Meyer, Vol II, pp. 351-398.

different forms of one primordial power. . . . In the winter
of 1819-20, he delivered a course of lectures upon electricity,
galvanism and magnetism, before an audience that had
been previously acquainted with the principles of natural
philosophy. In composing the lecture, in which he was to
treat of the analogy between magnetism and electricity, he
conjectured, that if it were possible to produce any magnetical effect by electricity, this could not be in the direction
of the current, since this had been so often tried in vain,
but that it must be produced by a lateral action. . . . As the
luminous and heating effect of the electrical current, goes
out in all directions from a conductor, which transmits a
great quantity of electricity; so he thought it possible that
the magnetical effect could likewise eradiate. . . . The plan
of the first experiment was, to make the current of a little
galvanic trough apparatus, commonly used in his lectures,
pass through a very thin platina wire, which was placed over
a compass covered with glass. The preparations for the experiments were made, but some accident having hindered
him from trying it before the lecture, he intended to defer
it to another opportunity; yet during the lecture, the prob-
ability of its success appeared stronger, so that he made the
first experiment in the presence of the audience. The magnetical needle, though included in a box, was disturbed;
but as the effect was very feeble, and must, before its law
was discovered, seem very irregular, the experiment made no
strong impression on the audience. It may appear strange,
that the discoverer made no further experiments upon the
subject during three months. . . . In the month of July
1820,* he again resumed the experiment, making use of a
much more considerable galvanical apparatus. The success
was now evident, yet the effects were still feeble in the first

---

* The text reads "1829," an obvious error

repetitions of the experiment, because he employed only very thin wires, supposing that the magnetical effect would not take place, when heat and light were not produced by the galvanical current; but he soon found that conductors of a greater diameter give much more effect; and he then discovered, by continued experiments during a few days, the fundamental law of electromagnetism, viz. *that the magnetical effect of the electrical current has a circular motion around it.''*

From this it seems quite clear that Oersted expected a magnetic effluent from this electrical wire in concert with the heat and the light which he knew would evolve from the glowing wire. He was conscious of the failure of previous experimenters, particularly Ritter, to observe any magnetism present, and that prompted considerable caution. In his attempt to reconcile the interaction of the new forces, he retained the idea of an "electrical conflict," meaning the discharge between opposite electricities that occurred along a spiral line about the axis of the conductor and the magnetism that surrounded it. He considered heat and light also to be manifestations of an electrical conflict, each accompanied by circular motions such as the demonstrable magnetic field around a current-carrying wire.

Another source of information as to what occurred, but remained unreported during the critical months of the spring and early summer, 1820, was a letter dated December 30, 1857, from a former pupil and friend of Oersted, Christopher Hansteen, writing to Faraday. According to this account, Oersted tried placing the wire of the battery perpendicular to the magnetic needle, but observed no

---

* Also quoted by Meyer, Vol II, pp. 356-8. It is to be noted that in none of his five accounts does Oersted give the month or day of the experiments.

motion. However, toward the end of a lecture, Oersted tried the wire parallel with the needle and saw the needle swing into a right-angle position. Oersted was then supposed to have inverted the direction of the current and to have seen the needle swing into an opposite position. However, this report was made 37 years after the event by one not present at the lecture. It is much more probable that, after the observation by Oersted of the first successful result, he waited three months in order to construct a more powerful battery and then, in July 1820, a series of experiments confirmed his original observation and he felt ready to announce his discovery.

In these later experiments, some sixty in number, he observed no decrease in magnetic effect even through screens of wood, glass, marble, clay, water, etc. Similarly, different kinds of wire to carry the current—platinum, gold, silver, brass, iron, ribbons of lead and tin, even a pool of mercury —all proved equally effective. Another impressive observa-

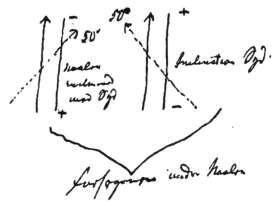

MEYER, vol I, p LXXXIV

To help celebrate the centenary of Oersted's discovery, Dr Kirstine Meyer of Copenhagen reviewed Oersted's unpublished laboratory notes of July 1820 with their scores of diagrams showing the action of electricity on a magnet One of these is shown above

tion was that made when the magnetism produced by the electric current acted upon a magnet being held in position by yet another magnet. Many manuscript notes of Oersted's experiments are dated throughout the first three weeks of July, and especially many occurred on July 15. No further time was to be lost before announcing the discovery.

The four-page announcement was transmitted on the day of publication to learned societies and scholars in all European countries. Further, Oersted continued his experiments and published the accumulating results in several journals.* In the very journal (Schweigger's) that first carried the text of Oersted's announcement, there already appeared descriptions of additional experiments under the title, "New Electro-Magnetic Research." It revealed that the magnetic effect of a conducting wire depended on the "quantity" of electricity and not on its "tension." Thus, a battery with larger plates would be more effective than one with small plates. Also, a suspended, closed, current-carrying loop might be turned by a magnet and such a loop had a north end and a south end, just like a magnet. This addendum may well be considered as a supplement to the original communication.† By using a cell consisting of a copper vessel

---

* Almost simultaneously the paper was translated into English in Thomson's *Annals of Philosophy*, Oct 1820, vol. xvi, pp. 274-275; into French, *Journal de Physique*, 1820, vol. xci, pp. 72-76; *Annales de Chimie et de Physique*, 1820, vol xiv, pp. 417-425; *Bibliothèque Universelle des Sciences*, 1820, vol. xiv, pp. 274-284; *Annales Générales des Sciences Physiques*, 1820, vol. v, pp. 259-264; into German, Gilbert's *Annalen der Physik*, 1820, vol. lxvi, pp. 295-304; Schweigger's *Journal fur Chemie und Physik*, 1820, vol xxix, pp 275-281; into Italian, *Giornale Arcadico di Scienze*, 1820, vol viii, pp. 174-178; Brugnatelli's *Giornale di Fisica*, 1820, pp. 335-342; into Danish, Hesperus. Udgivet af K L Rahbek III Bd pp 312-21, Kioebenhavn, 1820.

† Schweigger, *Journal fur Chemie und Physik*, July 1820, pp. 364-369

holding the electrolyte and immersing a zinc plate of 100-square-inch surface, Oersted was able to observe a magnetic effect at a distance of 3 feet.

Photo courtesy Danmarks Tekniske Hojskole

The actual magnetic compass used by Oersted in the revealing experiment of 1820 is still in the possession of the Polytechnic Institute of Copenhagen. It is shown resting on one of the very few surviving copies of the epochal announcement, in Latin, of his discovery of electromagnetism.

Once Oersted's discovery was exposed to the analytical minds of his fellow experimenters, a flood of new interpretations, modified procedures, and involved theories was advanced by many experimenters who were ready to treat their own remarks as though they were the prime discovery itself. Faraday attempted to bring some order into the mounting number of fresh announcements and reports of discoveries in the eight months following Oersted's disclosure. He gave clear and full credit to Oersted for his discovery, but even Faraday's voice was muted by the many new announcements and claims of the early 1820's. Some were ready to ride the bandwagon, others were equally ready to label Oersted's discovery just a lucky accident. Recognition of the importance of Oersted's discovery was spontaneous and was immediately followed by a shower of congratulations, honors, and awards. He was elected to fellowship in many learned societies and the Royal Society of London awarded him the Copley Medal; the Institut de France presented him with a prize of 3000 gold francs.

Ampère's Electrodynamics

Less than two months after the publication date of Oersted's announcement, news of his discovery had reached Paris via Geneva where Professor de la Rive repeated the Oersted experiment. This news was announced at a meeting of the Institut de France at a session held on Monday, September 11, 1820, at which André-Marie Ampère (1775-1836), professor of mathematics at the École Polytechnique, was present to listen to the announcement made by the great physicist, Arago. Ampère recognized the importance of the description of Oersted's experiment and, seven days later, presented a paper* at the Academie des Sciences; in this

---

* The paper by Ampère was entitled *Mémoire sur l'action mutuelle de deux courants électriques*, it was the first of five papers describing the action of conductors carrying electric currents in mutually attracting and repelling one another These comprised the fundamental laws of electrodynamics. Another paper, *Mémoire sur la théorie mathématique des phénomènes électrodynamiques*, presented by Ampère on October 2, was called by Maxwell "perfect in form and unassailable in accuracy."

paper, he mathematically analyzed Oersted's work and added some clarifying experiments of his own to prove that an electric current was capable of creating a full and true magnetic field. The positive position of a magnetic needle in its relation to an electric current was here first specified.

Burndy Library

ANDRÉ-MARIE AMPÈRE

The announcement of Oersted's important discovery of electromagnetism prompted Ampère, professor of mathematics in Paris, to formulate the laws of action between conductors carrying an electric current Attraction and repulsion were determined for straight and formed conductors, the magnetic behavior of solenoids explored, a galvanometer proposed and an electromagnetic telegraph indicated

This was then extended to conductors having spiral or helical shapes, indicating the cumulative values of the magnetic forces. Ampère then generalized a theory by which he analyzed the electromagnetic forces circulating within a magnetic molecule as the basis of its magnetic property. Philosophers thereby grasped the deep significance of providing man with a means of fashioning magnetic fields without dependence on lodestones or steel bars, for an easily controlled electric current now provided an even stronger form of magnet, as shown by Ampère. With this demonstration, Ampère had made the great leap forward, for he showed that not only could an electric current *influence* a magnet, but it was in itself capable of *producing* magnetism. He showed, further, that two solenoids carrying currents behaved like true magnets in polar attraction and repulsion. Until then, only the lodestone was held to be the source of magnetic power. A new and more powerful agency for creating magnetism had thus been discovered. By mathematical analysis, Ampère predicted electrodynamic behavior, subsequently proven by experiment.

It was said that, as Newton had formulated the laws of gravity and Coulomb, those of electrostatics, Ampère had now described and charted the laws of electrodynamics.

Arago, like Seebeck, was at the first reports skeptical of the Oersted claims, but then was prompted to remark that "the vast field of physical science perhaps never presented so brilliant a discovery, conceived, verified and completed with such rapidity." The able Faraday commented, "It is full of important matter and contains in few words, the results of a great number of observations; and with his second paper, comprises a very large part of the facts, that are as yet known relating to the subject" and "His constancy in the pursuit of his subject, both by reasoning and experiment, was well rewarded in the winter of 1819-1820 by the discovery of a fact of which not a single person beside himself had the slightest suspicion; but which, when once known, instantly drew the attention of all who were able to appreciate its importance and value."* To this, Ampère added, "M. Oersted has forever attached his name to a new epoch. . . . This learned Danish professor has opened, by his great discovery, a new approach for physical research."† Investigators everywhere soon busied themselves with the extension of magnetism to combined electrical and chemical experiments.

Experiments by Ampère had disclosed that when electric currents were passed in the same direction through two parallel wires free to move, they caused mutual attraction; if the currents flowed in opposite directions, the wires repelled one another. These observations provided the second law of electromagnetism.‡ Ampère determined the rules for relating the direction of flow of a current in a wire to the direction in which an adjoining compass needle would point, and illustrated it by a simple means so that it could be memorized. If, he stated, one were to imagine a little manikin (called a "bon homme d'Ampère" by Ampère's colleagues) to swim in the direction of the current and to face the needle, then the north pole of the needle would be the direction of the left arm and the south pole that of the right arm. The pointing of the needle could thereby be predicted and thus the experimenter acquired command of an additional set of electrophysical relationships with which to work. Ampère further determined that the force of the attraction or repulsion between current-carrying parallel wires would be directly proportional to the strength of the

---

* Quoted in Meisen, V., ed., *Prominent Danish Scientists*, Copenhagen, 1932, p. 93.

† In the *Journal de Physique*, 1822, quoted in Meisen, p. 93

‡ The first law is credited to Oersted and is to the effect that an electrical current generates a magnetic field circular to the flow of the electric current.

current and inversely proportional to the square of the distance between the wires.* Twisting the wire into a helical form, or solenoid, and having a current flow through it caused it to behave like a magnet having a north pole at one end and a south pole at the other. If such a coil were to be freely suspended and still carry current, it would pivot so that its magnetic field would align itself with the field of the earth's magnetism and so duplicate the behavior of a compass needle.

GRAETZ, p 159

A current-carrying loop was pivoted by Ampère free to move on its vertical axis The loop ends were set into mercury-filled cups and when the current was applied the loop moved until its electromagnetism coincided with that of earth's magnetism

---

* This discovery prompted Clerk Maxwell to call Ampère the "Newton of Electricity "

Ampère was led to the hypothesis that terrestrial currents of electricity circulating from east to west about the earth might be responsible for its magnetic field. From this came Ampère's proposal for the construction of an astatic galvanometer* to negate the stray magnetism in the measurement of an electric current. Ampère repeated, on October 2, 1820, the suggestion made by Laplace that the response of a magnetic needle to a current-carrying wire could be made the principle of an electromagnetic telegraph. One had simply to identify a needle with a letter and by energizing the wire adjacent to a particular needle, the desired letter could be so indicated. The theory was good, but the practice, as in the case of the Soemmering chemical telegraph, never became practical because of the complexity of wires.

The first practical application of Oersted's discovery was by Johann S. C. Schweigger, who announced on September 16, 1820, his improvement of a galvano-magnetic indicator which he called a "multiplier." This consisted of a coil of insulated wire of several turns about a magnetic needle. It was found to indicate quantitatively the magnetic force generated by the amount of current flowing in the coil. Schweigger had also observed that the deflecting power on the needle was increased by increasing the number of turns. Dr. Thomas J. Seebeck (1770-1831) experimenting with this indicator (or galvanometer) came to the conclusion that the effective power of a current flowing in a coil was not directly dependent on the number of turns because increasing the number of turns increased the length, and therefore the resistance, of the wire and decreased the resulting conductive

---

* This invention is sometimes credited to Professor James Cumming's paper *On the Connection of Galvanism and Magnetism*, read at Cambridge in 1821, and to the improvement by Leopoldo Nobili in 1825

power. The first electrical measuring instrument, based on the new electromagnetic force, was thus created.*

During 1820, Davy had noticed that iron filings had adhered to a current-carrying wire to form a mass of ten or twelve times the thickness of the conductor. The same phenomenon was observed by Arago and Seebeck in differing forms, using filings, soft iron and steel needles. They found that the soft iron ones were difficult to magnetize permanently, but the steel ones retained their magnetism permanently.

Romagnosi and Mojon

As early as 1774, the Academy of Bavaria had offered a prize for the best dissertation in answer to the question "Is there a real and physical analogy between electric and magnetic forces?" Professor J. H. van Swinden of Holland replied, in conclusion, that the similarities were entirely superficial and that the two forces were essentially of a different kind. A contrary position was taken by Professors Steighlehner and Hubner in 1773 and 1780 that such related forces must have their origin in a single agent. The full resolution of the question continues into our own time.

Two years after the voltaic pile had been announced, there appeared a letter in the *Gazzetta di Trento*, Italy, on

---

* Johann C. Poggendorff of Berlin modified Schweigger's galvanometer by having a vertical helix draw an unmagnetized needle, and published his results before Schweigger's account appeared, although Schweigger's device preceded the independent device of Poggendorff

August 3, 1802, in which Gian Domenico Romagnosi (1761-1835) a local jurist and amateur physicist of Trent and the university at Parma, described an electrical experiment that he had performed. Romagnosi's account,* in translation, reads as follows:

ARTICLE ON GALVANISM

The Counsellor, Gian Domenico de Romagnosi of this city, known to the republic of letters by his learned productions, hastens to communicate to the physicists of Europe an experiment showing the action of the galvanic fluid on magnetism.

Having constructed a voltaic pile, of thin discs of copper and zinc, separated by flannel soaked in a solution of sal-ammoniac, he attached to one of the poles one end of a silver chain. the other end of which passed through a short glass tube, and terminated in a silver knob. This being done, he took an ordinary compass-box, placed it on a glass stand, removed its glass cover, and touched one end of the needle with the silver knob, which he took care to hold by its glass envelope. After a few seconds' contact, the needle was observed to take up a new position, where it remained, even after the removal of the knob. A fresh application of the knob caused a still further deflection of the needle, which was always observed to remain in the position to which it was last deflected, as if its polarity were altogether destroyed.

In order to restore this polarity, Romagnosi took the compass-box between his fingers and thumbs, and held it steadily for some seconds. The needle then returned to its original position, not all at once, but little by little, advancing like the minute or seconds hand of a clock.

These experiments were made in the month of May, and repeated in the presence of a few spectators, when the effect was obtained without trouble and at a very sensible distance.

---

* From Fahie, *A History of Electric Telegraphy*, 1884, p 259.

MISSIRINI, 1840

GIAN DOMENICO ROMAGNOSI

Jurist and physicist, his experiment with a voltaic cell and magnetic compass
came close, but failed, to lead to electromagnetic discovery.†

† In Hamel's engaging book of 1859, there appears, on page 39, the
request: "In Alessandro de Giorgi's collection of the works of Romagnosi,
printed at Milan, there is prefixed to the first volume a likeness of him,
engraved from a painting by Ernesta Bisi. I wish somebody would copy it
by photographic means, and then multiply this portrait by the same process,
for distribution among the lovers of the electrical science." May the ghost
of Hamel forgive the delay of a century.

Romagnosi did not subsequently expand on the experiment* nor did he draw any general conclusions from it,

---

* Gilberto Govi published a paper in 1869, *Romagnosi e l'Elettro-
Magnetismo*, Torino, from which he concluded that the attraction and
repulsion observed by Romagnosi must have been electrostatic and not
electromagnetic.

thus missing the chance of discovering electromagnetism.

Benedetto Mojon of Genoa reported an experiment in 1804 in which he placed steel needles in a circuit of a voltaic battery and let them remain there for many days. Mojon observed that the needles were magnetized when removed from the circuit. Like Romagnosi, Mojon did not expand on the experiment and also drew no basic conclusions. Romagnosi, who died in 1835, never claimed priority over Oersted in the 15 years subsequent to the announcement on electromagnetism in 1820 by the latter.

Obscure as the Romagnosi notice in the *Gazzetta* was, it was shortly picked up and repeated in two books by authors of considerable prominence. In 1804 Giovanni Aldini* (1762-1834) published a large quarto of nearly 400 pages (dedicated to Napoleon) in which, on page 191, he alluded to the supposed magnetic influence of a galvanic circuit by stating, "This new property of galvanism has been confirmed by M. Romanesi, a physicist of Trent, who has observed that galvanism produces a declination of the magnetic needle."†

On page 338 of Aldini's book, an addendum of two and a half pages reviewed the relationship of electricity and magnetism which, he then pointed out, one already knew. The beautiful experiments of d'AEpinus, van Swinden, Cavallo, and Coulomb proved the close connection that existed between the two fluids. Lightning in striking a ship had been known to change the magnetic poles of the compass, which demonstrated the influence of electricity on magnetism. "I have believed it expedient to expose this

---

* Aldini, Jean, *Essai Théorique et Expérimental sur le Galvanisme,* Paris, 1804

† During the same year, and also in Paris, the same work was republished in two volumes, octavo, where the quotation was repeated on page 339 of Volume I

last principle to the action of Galvanic apparatus," promised Aldini. He then described how he used a pile of 40 discs of copper and an equal number of zinc, each being three inches in diameter but having a central hole $1\frac{1}{2}$ inches in diameter so as to form a pile that had a hollow core. Into this he could insert steel needles to see if they could become magnetized, or to change the polarity of other needles already magnetized. "My results were so weak that I do not dare to draw a single decisive conclusion from them. They were a little more satisfactory when I left the needles exposed for a very long time to the current of a strong pile." But oxidation and the continued changing of soiled parts of the equipment prevented him from arriving at any definite conclusions. He then related how M. Mojon placed fine sewing needles 2 inches long horizontally between the terminals of a battery of a hundred cups where they remained for 20 days. These became oxidized but also magnetized with sensitive polarity. He then referred to the procedure of magnetizing by means of galvanism as had already been established by "Romanesi," who had caused a magnetic needle to decline by the application of current from a voltaic pile. Franklin had magnetized needles by using the discharge of four Leyden jars, as reported by Priestley in 1767.

The second popular work on galvanism was that of Professor Joseph Izarn* which also appeared in Paris in 1804. This included instructions given for magnetizing needle as proposed by Romagnosi† of Trent and Mojon of Genoa.

---

* Professor of Physics at the Lycée Bonaparte The book's title was *Manuel du Galvanisme.*

† The Romagnosi experiment was reviewed in Zantedeschi, F *Trattato del Magnetismo e della Elettricità*, Venezia, 1846, Vol II, p. 2.

"*Effects*—According to the observations of Romagnési, physicist of Trent, a needle already magnetized and which one thus submits to the galvanic current, shows a declination; and according to those of J. Mojon, a learned chemist of Genoa, the needles not magnetized acquire by this means a sort of magnetic polarity." This book was among those that were required, by order, to be placed in the library of every lycée in France.

120 MANUEL DU GALVANISME.

§. I X.

Appareil pour reconnaître l'action du Galvanisme , sur la polarité d'une aiguille aimantée.

Préparation. Disposez les tiges horisontales *a b*, *b d* de l'appareil (*fig.* 53), de manière que les deux boutons se trouvent à une distance un peu moindre que la longueur des aiguilles que vous voudrez soumettre à l'expérience ; et, à la place des boutons *b b* , qui sont vissés sur leur tige respective, adaptez aux tiges, ou une petite pince, ou bien un petit ajutage applati.

Usage. Après avoir placé l'aiguille, de manière que ses deux extrémités soient prises dans les deux petites pinces ; établissez une communication de *d* , avec une des extrémités d'un Electromoteur, et de *a*, avec l'extrémité opposée.

Effets. D'après les observations de Romagnési, physicien de Trente, l'aiguille déjà aimentée , et que l'on soumet ainsi au courant galvanique , éprouve une déclinaison; et , d'après celles de J. Mojon, savant chimiste de Gènes , les aiguilles non-aimentées acquièrent , par ce moyen, une sorte de polarité magnétique.

IZARN, p 120

Procedure for determining the action of galvanism on a magnetic needle was outlined by Izarn in 1804 References to the observations by Romagnosi and Mojon are indicated in the last paragraph.

[47]

A study was made by Dr. Joseph J. Hamel* of St. Petersburg as to the failure of both Dr. Soemmering and Baron Schilling to take note of the description of Romagnosi's important discovery, as reported in the above two books. Dr. Hamel concluded that when Schilling returned to Munich in 1815, he communicated with Soemmering about the book by Izarn. Hamel also reported seeing a note from Soemmering, indicating that he had read the treatise with attention. However, both investigators failed to grasp the practical implications of the note on Romagnosi and Mojon.

To some, it appears that even the announcement of Oersted's discovery need not necessarily have led directly to the development of the electromagnet and electromagnetic telegraphy, for the contributions of Schweigger, Ampère, Arago, Sturgeon, Henry, and Morse seemed essential additional contributions. Dr. Hamel had added, "Hans Christian Oersted, at Copenhagen, had directed the attention of the scientific world, much more effectually than Romagnosi, in Italy had done, to the fact that the magnetic needle deflects, when a galvanic current comes near it.† The conclusion is therefore drawn that Romagnosi's observation was not thoroughly investigated, but was inadequately reported and made at a time when the world of science seemed unprepared to appreciate the vast significance of his observation or to apply it as was done immediately after the Oersted announcement. Like the parable of the seed, the one was an early sowing that fell upon a stony place, the other, made in the full spring and falling on rich soil, took root and

---

* Dr Hamel's remarks appeared in the Journal of the Society of Arts, London, for July 29, 1859, and are repeated in a reprint in November 1859 under the title, *Historical Account of the Introduction of the Galvanic and Electro-Magnetic Telegraph into England*

† Hamel, p. 35

flowered. Oersted's love of the world of nature and his broad interests in science and philosophy tended to guide him to unifying forces and common laws binding related phenomena.

It must also be noted that a basic difference existed between a circuit similar to one constructed by Mojon, in which an iron needle was inserted in the circuit and found to become magnetized, and that of Oersted, in which the needle was near, but not in, the electrical circuit. One (even if clearly understood) does not lead to the other. In fact, a contrary effect was reported by Oersted in his article on

FAHIE, p 260

Romagnosi's experiment with the influence of a voltaic pile on a magnetic needle was interpreted by Govi (1869) as an electrostatic, rather than an electromagnetic, effect

"Thermo-Electricity" (see page 30); a Mr. Hill of Lund, Sweden, found that when a discharge passed *along* a magnetic needle, all its magnetism was destroyed.* Oersted's was obviously an independent and basically different approach, one that led directly to the recognition and formulation of the laws of electromagnetism.

Dr. Hamel also examined the question of whether Oersted might already have known of Romagnosi's account.

тело ток в землю, можно было объяснить этот опыт. Это и сделал соотечественник Романьози Зантедески в 1859 г , но, не

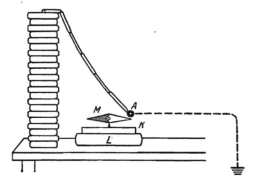

Рис. 1

ограничиваясь разъяснением приведенной нами заметки, он необоснованно выдвинул тезис о приоритете Романьози в открытии электромагнетизма и существования «открытых» токов, распространяющихся через Землю⁹.

The continuing interest in the Romagnosi experiment is represented in a recent study by Professor Olga Lezhneva of the U S S R Academy of Sciences on the early history of electromagnetism It is supposed that grounding through the experimenter's body might have completed the circuit and permitted the flow of enough current to affect the needle

---

* Published in Schweigger's *Journal*, No 3 for 1822

While it was true that Oersted had been in Paris in 1802 and 1803, and in contact with Aldini through correspondence, yet would he have waited 18 years to repeat the electromagnetic experiment, let alone expand on it, or chance someone else's announcement of so vital a combination? Besides, it is noted that Oersted's generous, open, and upright character must preclude any such deviousness, although Hamel did wish that, "on making known his own observations, he had just said a word about Romagnosi as pioneer in the field on which he became loaded with laurels."* Hamel was indeed generous, but not as understanding as Govi.† Dr. Hamel spoke with considerable authority because he was personally acquainted with Oersted, Schweigger, Ampère, Arago, Soemmering, Schilling, and the other founders of electromagnetic science and telegraphic practices.

Applied Electromagnetism

Schilling reduced the telegraphic problem in 1823 to an installation in St. Petersburg of an electromagnetic telegraph apparatus employing five galvanometer needles, each having its own independent galvanic circuit. Introducing the ingenious expedient of causing each needle to move either positively or negatively, resorting to a reversal of currents, and combining two or more of these signals allowed a great simplification of the alphabet. This apparatus was

---

* Hamel, p. 39.
† See the footnote on p 44

exhibited to the Emperor Alexander I shortly before his death in 1825.

In early February 1823, Oersted was in Paris where he spent much time with Ampère, Arago, Fresnel, and Fourier. While Oersted was there, announcement arrived of the dis-

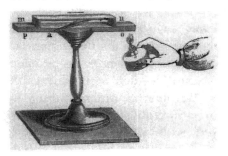

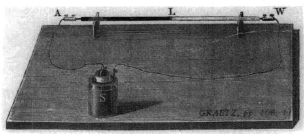

The Seebeck effect resulted when one end of a couple consisting of two joined dissimilar metals (here, bismuth and copper) was heated. An electric current, as manifested by the rotated needle, was generated. An opposite condition, the Peltier effect, was created when an electric current was passed through two joined, dissimilar metals (here, iron and copper) thereby warming the junction, or cooling it when the current flow was reversed. In our present hunt for new approaches to more efficient electric generation, these discoveries of nearly a century and a half ago are again being investigated.

covery made by Seebeck of the Royal Academy in Berlin. Seebeck showed that a plate of copper and one of bismuth, when pressed together by a finger at one end, produced a deflection on a galvanometer connected to the other end of the couple. Oersted immediately saw in this an additional bridge joining differing kinds of physical forces. He then began a series of experiments from which he found that a combination of bismuth and antimony gave improved results. He and Baron Fourier thereupon proposed that a multiplication of alternate strips of bismuth and antimony be joined into a ring so that heat could be applied at every second junction, leaving the first junction at room temperature; cooling the second with ice seemed to produce an even stronger electrical effect. Combining the heating at one end and cooling at the other caused the compass to deflect 60 degrees. This system would correspond to the assembly, and therefore its effects would be similar to the effects, of plates forming a voltaic pile. Oersted proposed the name "thermo-electric" for the currents so generated and published the results in a joint communication with Fourier in the *Annales de Chimie et Physique,* Volume XXII, Paris, 1823. Jean Peltier demonstrated in 1834 that the passage of an electric current through two joined dissimilar metals created or absorbed heat at the juncture, depending on the direction of current flow.

Oersted's contribution to the separation of aluminum was communicated in mid February, 1825, to the Royal Society of Sciences. In this, he reported success in procuring a compound of chlorine and the combustible portion of alumina to which he had applied hydrogen. Over a mixture of carbon and pure alumina, which was heated to incandescence in a china tube, Oersted passed dry chlorine. Oxygen was emitted and aluminum chloride formed. This was quickly heated with potassium amalgam which decomposed into potassium chloride and aluminum amalgam. Distillation without admitting air produced metallic aluminum, a sample of which he showed in April to the Society of Sciences. A report on this appeared in Poggendorff's

*Annalen der Physik.** In spite of this, credit for the initial
production of aluminum is generally ascribed to Wöhler,
whose paper was published in 1827. In this, he indicated
that he had read of Oersted's experiments. The clearer
account by Wöhler, however, fixed the latter's method more
definitely in men's minds.

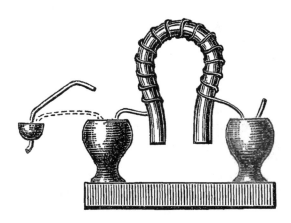

FAHIE, p 286

Sturgeon, in 1825, wound 16 turns of bare copper on a varnished soft
iron core   When current was switched through, the resulting magnet
lifted nine pounds, or 20 times its weight, a prodigious accomplishment for
the first electromagnet

The next important step in the evolution of electromagnetic theory and apparatus was that made by William
Sturgeon (1783-1850) of England who, in 1825, wound an
electric wire in sixteen turns around a soft iron core and so
produced an electromagnet. He found soft iron to be better

---

* Volume V, Leipzig, 1825, p. 132

than steel because it was capable of stronger temporary magnetism than steel. This was true only while the current was flowing, soft iron lacking the retentivity of steel. Sturgeon bent the iron core into a horseshoe shape, thereby bringing the poles into the same plane and further intensifying the magnetism, as well as making its influence upon an iron object more convenient. The conductor he used was bare wire wound around the soft iron core which had been heavily varnished so as to insulate the successive turns of the bare conducting wire. This electromagnet had distinct advantages over a lodestone: strong lifting power, instantaneous magnetization, immediate ending of the magnetic field when the circuit was opened, and the ease with which the electromagnet could be positioned anywhere.

To Joseph Henry, teacher and experimenter at Albany, New York, goes the credit for masterful work in exploiting these properties. Instead of varnishing the iron core, he concentrated on providing an insulating cover upon the conductor itself. He used a silk winding about the copper wire and thus could closely pack many turns upon the iron core. This he demonstrated at the Albany Institute in June 1828. To one small magnet he applied 35 feet of wire in 400 turns and showed the improved properties of such a magnet in the following year. As a next step, he wound two layers of turns about a core, connecting the coil ends at each pole end, thus joining the coils in parallel. The resulting pull was nearly doubled. This opened the general field of inquiry to Henry, a mathematics teacher, as to which variables—number of turns, size of wire, kind of battery, number and method of connection of coils—were those from which the optimum condition of magnetic strength was to be determined. He found that, with the current from a single pair of zinc and copper plates only one inch square, he could construct a magnet to sustain 85 pounds of iron. With a

FAHIE, p 292

Joseph Henry insulated the wire of his electromagnets with silk, compacted them with many turns, and connected the coils in parallel and in series, increasing the suspended weights to over a ton With this apparatus* he discovered self-induction The battery, reversing switch, and ribbon-coil which he built are shown on the floor

* Copied from the December 11, 1880 issue of *Scientific American*

single cell of less than half a square foot of surface, 650 pounds could be sustained. In 1831, he built a magnet having an iron core weighing less than 60 pounds, yet it was capable of holding up more than a ton. Another magnet which Henry made held up 3600 pounds. Thus, in about a decade after the announcement of the principle of electromagnetism, an electric battery, no larger than the one that first showed Oersted its magnetic property, was used to sustain a weight of a ton.

Electromagnetic Induction

Three events provided the stable base of modern electrical science: the discovery of a constant-current source of electricity by Volta, the magnetic influence of an electric current by Oersted and, finally, the generation of an electric current from magnetism by Faraday.

Ever since Oersted's announcement that magnetism could be generated by electricity, the hunt for the reciprocal condition, the generation of electricity from a magnetic source, became the goal of experimenters. Michael Faraday (1791-1867), of most humble beginnings, was assistant to Sir Humphry Davy at the Royal Institution and, because of his brilliance as an experimenter, became one of the immortals of science. For ten years, he had worked on the problem of conversion of a magnetic force into electricity, but without success. However, on August 29, 1831, he observed that when two coils were wound around a common core and one was connected to an electric battery, the making and breaking of the electric current in the first coil created a kindred pulse of electricity in the second coil of the circuit in which a galvanometer had been inserted. Thus, electromagnetic induction was discovered.

As a further step in following this discovery, Faraday, on October 28, 1831, mounted a copper disk so that it could be made to revolve between the pole ends of a powerful magnet. Galvanometer leads were then connected, one to the axle of the revolving disk and the second to the disk's edge. When the disk was turned by a crank, the galvanometer needle deflected, clearly showing that electric currents had been induced in the disk. The first dynamo-electric machine had been born. The electrical age was now pos-

M Oersted
L L LL
from the author

EXPERIMENTAL RESEARCHES

IN

E L E C T R I C I T Y.

(Eighteenth Series)

§ 25 *On the electricity evolved by the friction of water and steam against other bodies*

BY

MICHAEL FARADAY, Esq, D C L F R S,

Fullerian Prof Chem Royal Institution Corr Memb Royal and Imp Acadd of Sciences Paris, Petersburgh Florence Copenhagen Berlin Göttingen Modena Stockholm &c &c

From the PHILOSOPHICAL TRANSACTIONS —Part I ros 1843

LONDON

PRINTED BY RICHARD AND JOHN E TAYLOR, RED LION COURT, FLEET STREET

1843

Burndy Library

Oersted's discovery of the magnetic effects of an electric current was matched by Faraday's discovery of electricity generated from magnetism, disclosed in a brilliant series of 30 papers to the Royal Society Above, a copy that he sent to Oersted

sible. In ten days of intensive experimentation, Faraday had grasped and formulated the basic laws of magneto-electric generation. His results were presented in the first of a long series of papers before the Royal Society on November 24, 1831. To the chemical source of electric generation of Volta, there was added the magneto-electric form of generation by Faraday. Mechanical energy was now convertible into electrical energy. By adding the concept of the magnetic field with its lines of force (as dramatically demonstrable with iron filings), Faraday physically linked the elements that engaged in magneto-electric generation.

The principle of self-induction was first observed by Professor Henry in 1832 with the apparatus shown on the illustration on page 56. With this apparatus, he obtained a brilliant spark when he opened a circuit connecting an electric battery to a coil of copper wire. This occurred when he quickly broke the circuit by using a copper jumper joining two cups of mercury in the circuit. From his experiments, he concluded that in order to obtain this spark it was necessary for the length of wire to exceed 12 or 14 yards. An even better effect resulted when the wire was coiled into a helix.

The Electromagnetic Telegraph

Building on Oersted's discovery of electromagnetism, Ampère was probably the first to suggest this new force as the means of transmitting signals over an electric wire. This suggestion was the foundation for our modern telegraphic system. Ampère argued that if a needle could be deflected by an electric current, then this motion could be converted by code into an alphabetic system. The practical application of this arrangement failed, like the earlier electrochemical proposals, because the number of wires required proved too unwieldy. However, Sturgeon's electromagnet gave new impetus to the inventors in telegraphy. Various needle telegraphs were invented, promoted and shelved. In 1834 Gauss and Weber drew a $1\frac{1}{4}$-mile-long telegraph line over the rooftops of Göttingen between the laboratory and observatory. Double wires connected magnetic indicating needles, and the line continued in use for four years until it was struck by lightning. It was improved by Steinheil who substituted a single wire and ground return. The English experimenters William F. Cooke and Charles Wheatstone expanded Schweigger's idea into an operating telegraph.

The telegraphic art received its final impetus from S. F. B. Morse who combined the primary elements of Sturgeon and Henry into a practical telegraph system, and then promoted its construction and use until it became, in its day, the universal means of long-range communication. With support from Congress in March 1843, a telegraph line between Washington and Baltimore was constructed by Morse, one that proved feasible.

Oersted and Faraday first met in London during the former's visit to England in 1823. They remained in correspondence for nearly 30 years and met again during Oersted's later visits to London. On Oersted's second visit to Faraday's laboratory in 1846 he expressed very great interest in the large horseshoe electromagnet that Faraday had constructed and with which he had conducted experiments in diamagnetism. When Oersted returned to Copenhagen he built a large electromagnet after Faraday's design; this still is preserved at the Polytechnic Institute. Demonstrations with it were made by Oersted before the Royal

Academy in Copenhagen for the two years 1847 to 1849, mostly in experiments with diamagnetism. Correspondence between the two savants covered the fields of the compressibility of fluids, the confirmation of Mariotte's law, the liquefaction of gases, and the continuation of Chladni's patterns of sound produced on vibrating plates.

Oersted's paper on the acoustical figures was written in 1807 (published 1810) and won for him the silver medal of the Royal Society of Sciences. It was an expansion of a letter to Ritter written in October 1804, and was in substance an electrical analysis of Chladni's figures. Oersted replaced Chladni's sand with a lighter powdered moss (lycopodium) and obtained a pattern of figures different from those of Chladni. Oersted had hoped to discover a relationship between parts of the acoustical figures with electrical charges, a further indication of his aim to correlate various manifestations of the forces of nature.

Scientist and Citizen

Absorbing the honors which came to him following the recognition of his discovery, Oersted threw himself into broadening the field of science education. He founded a society for the dissemination of scientific knowledge which has continued its mission into the present, and he delivered lectures on science in the principal cities of Denmark. In 1823-4, he continued these lectures but gave them in French. In 1828 he traveled to Norway and, in the same year, addressed a science society in Berlin. In the following years, he

again visited Hamburg and in 1834 called upon the celebrated electricians and experimenters in Göttingen, Gauss
and Weber, who had established a magnetic observatory
there. Oersted later established a similar magnetic study at
the Polytechnic Institute of Copenhagen on the ramparts of
the city. France and England were visited by Oersted in
1836 and he was among those present at the meeting of the
British Association at Southampton where he listened to Sir
John Herschel state that "in science there was but one direction which the needle would take, when pointed towards the
European continent, and that was towards his esteemed
friend, Professor Oersted. He knew not how to speak of him
in his presence without violating some of that sanctity by
which, as an individual, he was surrounded. . . . The electric
telegraph, and other wonders of modern science, were but
mere effervescences from the surface of this deep recondite
discovery which Oersted had liberated, and which was yet
to burst with all its mighty force upon the world. If we
were to characterize by any figure the advantage of Oersted
to science, we would regard him as a fertilizing shower
descending from heaven, which brought forth a new crop,
delightful to the eye and pleasing to the heart."*

In England he got to know his experimenting colleagues
Wollaston, Sir Humphry Davy, Michael Faraday, David
Brewster, and Sir Roderick Murchison, the geologist. On
returning home, he became secretary to the Royal Society
of Sciences in Copenhagen† and a director of the Royal
Polytechnic Institute which he had founded in 1829 as a
result of the impressions made upon King Frederik VI; this

---

* Quoted by Munro, *Pioneers of Electricity*, p 151.

† In 1842, while Oersted was still secretary of the Society, King
Christian VIII became its president and occasionally held the chair
during its meetings

college still continues as the primary source of engineering education for Denmark. Of the many honors granted Oersted, the one he treasured most was the award of the Grand Cross of the Dannebrog in 1847.

The first meeting between Hans Christian Oersted and his compatriot, Hans Christian Andersen (1805-1875), oc-

Courtesy A. Boje, Copenhagen

Anders *Oersted* *Sofie* *Oersted Dahlstrom*	*F. C.* *Dahlstrom* *H. C.* *Oersted*	*Karen Oersted* *Scharling* *Inger Birgitte* *Oersted*	*Edward* *Scharling*	*A. Nicolai* *Oersted* *Anders S.* *Oersted*

A daguerreotype of the Oersted family made in the late 1840's showing H. C. Oersted, his wife and jurist brother Anders S., two sons and two daughters.

curred when Andersen was 14. He arrived in Copenhagen as a poor boy and introduced himself to Oersted. He wrote later, "It was like a divine sign that I should turn to the most generous and best, to those whose importance I really did not know or was able to appreciate. From the very first moment and with continuously growing sympathy, which during his later years grew into true friendship, Oersted concerned himself about me unto his death . . . his house became very early a home for me; his children, when they were small, I have played with, seen them grow up and keep their love for me. In his home I have found my eldest and unchanged friends." On a certain day of every week, Andersen dined in the Oersted home and this tradition was continued by Mrs. Oersted for 24 years after her husband's death. Andersen took impish delight in referring to Oersted as the "Great Hans Christian," and to himself and the "Little Hans Christian."*

Oersted pursued his mission for science to which he was so deeply dedicated by every channel open to him. His lectures, including a series of popular lectures to ladies, covered many fields of science. In 1829, he founded a monthly journal of literature to which he contributed many essays in science. These were subsequently gathered in book form and published in Danish and in English under the title,

---

* I am indebted to Mr Andreas Boje of Copenhagen for supplying me with an account of some episodes in the private life of Oersted These include his stay with his brother at the home of his father's sister, the widow Aunt Engelke Moller, the deep bond of sympathy between Oersted and Andersen, and the courtship of Oersted with Inger Ballum, his future bride These notes were edited by Joergen Hertz, one of Oersted's descendants. Oersted's youngest daughter, Matilda, became Hans Christian Andersen's protégé and on the passing of Oersted's old friend, she was bequeathed the manuscripts of his world-famous stories.

Burndy Library

H C OERSTED TO H C ANDERSEN

Among Oersted's many friends, one of the closest was Hans Christian Andersen whom he befriended as a poor boy The above letter from Oersted to the great story teller concerns an invitation to Dr Lund to dine with them and attend a lecture by Oersted It was sent from Rudkoebing, Oersted's birthplace

[65]

The Soul in Nature, London, 1852. As a result of continued study, correspondence, and travel, he became fluent in German, French, Latin, and English in addition to his native Danish. He helped in the founding of a society for the promotion of the freedom of the press. In November 1850 the jubilee of the association of Oersted with the University of Copenhagen was celebrated as a national holiday. The King

Photo courtesy Danmarks Tekniske Hojskole

A photo portrait of H. C. Oersted taken in the late 1840's. The first announcement of photography was made in 1839 and Oersted died in 1851. The above photograph was therefore taken during the first dozen years of the practice of photography.

sent a deputation of ministers; professors and students joined the public in their congratulations to one of Denmark's greatest citizens. The government gave Oersted a country house near Copenhagen which had formerly been occupied by his old friend, the writer Oehlenschlaeger. A procession of students bearing torchlights proceeded to welcome him in his new home; they came singing verses in his praise as they marched.

But these honors were to be short-lived for on March 9, 1851 he died. The students bore his remains at night, again by torchlight, to the old university, chanting verses composed for this sad occasion. The King was represented in the funeral procession, and the crown prince, along with ministers and foreign ambassadors, showed the high esteem in which Oersted was held. Over 200,000 people joined in the procession.

Burndy Library

A medal awarded by the American Association of Physics Teachers shows Oersted demonstrating electromagnetism. This discovery, according to Professors George Sarton and I. B. Cohen, was the only instance of a great discovery having been made during a lecture demonstration.

As we face the nuclear age we can note the progress in the expansion of our knowledge of electromagnetism, and use it as an index of general science. Electromagnetism has become the major force in the generation, distribution, and use of electricity, our most useful aid.

No ancient seer could have prophesied man's ability to control such enormous blocks of power, such integration of networks covering such vast land areas, or put to such a wide order of usefulness. No dreamer could have anticipated obtaining such a delicacy of control, or the extension of man's limited faculties by acquiring electrical devices like the telephone, the cinema, television, the electron microscope, or radar astronomy. All had their beginnings in the discovery of electromagnetism.

Now there is scheduled a research project at the M.I.T. Magnet Laboratory to produce intense magnetic fields to help understand the nature of matter and energy by learning even more about electricity and magnetism. Available to this ten-million-dollar research project will be 32,000 kilowatts of electric power, enough to provide the full needs of some cities.

Oersted's hunt for interrelationships between the forces of nature has been picked up by the younger investigators in succeeding generations. Such hunger for greater knowledge continues to distinguish man from his fellow creatures.

Appendix

The Text of Oersted's Announcement of His Discovery of Electromagnetism

Reprinted from *Annals of Philosophy*, Volume 16, 1820

Appendix

*Experiments on the Effect of a Current of Electricity on the Magnetic Needle.** By John Christian Oersted, Knight of the Order of Danneborg, Professor of Natural Philosophy, and Secretary to the Royal Society of Copenhagen.

The first experiments respecting the subject which I mean at present to explain, were made by me last winter, while lecturing on electricity, galvanism, and magnetism, in the University. It seemed demonstrated by these experiments that the magnetic needle was moved from its position by the galvanic apparatus, but that the galvanic circle must be complete, and not open, which last method was tried in vain some years ago by very celebrated philosophers. But as these experiments were made with a feeble apparatus, and were not, therefore, sufficiently conclusive, considering the importance of the subject, I associated myself with my friend Esmarck to repeat and extend them by means of a very powerful galvanic battery, provided by us in common. Mr. Wleugel, a Knight of the Order of Danneborg, and at the head of the Pilots, was present at, and assisted in, the experi-

---

* Translated from a printed account drawn up in Latin by the author, and transmitted by him to the Editor of the *Annals of Philosophy*.

ments. There were present likewise Mr. Hauch, a man very well skilled in the Natural Sciences, Mr. Reinhardt, Professor of Natural History, Mr. Jacobsen, Professor of Medicine, and that very skilful chemist, Mr. Zeise, Doctor of Philosophy. I had often made experiments by myself; but every fact which I had observed was repeated in the presence of these gentlemen.

The galvanic apparatus which we employed consists of 20 copper throughs, the length and height of each of which was 12 inches; but the breadth scarcely exceeded 2½ inches. Every trough is supplied with two plates of copper, so bent that they could carry a copper rod, which supports the zinc plate in the water of the next trough. The water of the troughs contained 1/60th of its weight of sulphuric acid, and an equal quantity of nitric acid. The portion of each zinc plate sunk in the water is a square whose side is about 10 inches in length. A smaller apparatus will answer provided it be strong enough to heat a metallic wire red hot.

The opposite ends of the galvanic battery were joined by a metallic wire, which, for shortness sake, we shall call the *uniting conductor,* or the *uniting wire.* To the effect which takes place in this conductor and in the surrounding space, we shall give the name of the *conflict of electricity.*

Let the straight part of this wire be placed horizontally above the magnetic needle, properly suspended, and parallel to it. If necessary, the uniting wire is bent so as to assume a proper position for the experiment. Things being in this state, the needle will be moved, and the end of it next the negative side of the battery will go westward.

If the distance of the uniting wire does not exceed three-quarters of an inch from the needle, the declination of the needle makes an angle of about 45°. If the distance is increased, the angle diminishes proportionally. The declination likewise varies with the power of the battery.

The uniting wire may change its place, either towards the east or west, provided it continue parallel to the needle, without any other change of the effect than in respect to its quantity. Hence the effect cannot be ascribed to attraction; for the same pole of the magnetic needle, which approaches the uniting wire, while placed on its east side, ought to recede from it when on the west side, if these declinations depended on attractions and repulsions. The uniting conductor may consist of several wires, or metallic ribbons, connected together. The nature of the metal does not alter the effect, but merely the quantity. Wires of platinum, gold, silver, brass, iron, ribbons of lead and tin, a mass of mercury, were employed with equal success. The conductor does not lose its effect, though interrupted by water, unless the interruption amounts to several inches in length.

The effect of the uniting wire passes to the needle through glass, metals, wood, water, resin, stoneware, stones; for it is not taken away by interposing plates of glass, metal or wood Even glass, metal, and wood, interposed at once, do not destroy, and indeed scarcely diminish the effect. The disc of the electrophorus, plates of porphyry, a stone-ware vessel, even filled with water, were interposed with the same result. We found the effects unchanged when the needle was included in a brass box filled with water. It is needless to observe that the transmission of effects through all these matters has never before been observed in electricity and galvanism. The effects, therefore, which take place in the conflict of electricity are very different from the effects of either of the electricities.

If the uniting wire be placed in a horizontal plane under the magnetic needle, all the effects are the same as when it is above the needle, only they are in an opposite direction: for the pole of the magnetic needle next the negative end of the battery declines to the east.

That these facts may be the more easily retained, we may use this formula—the pole *above* which the *negative* electricity enters is turned to the *west; under* which, to the *east.*

If the uniting wire is so turned in a horizontal plane as to form a gradually increasing angle with the magnetic meridian, the declination of the needle *increases,* if the motion of the wire is towards the place of the disturbed needle; but it *diminishes* if the wire moves further from that place.

When the uniting wire is situated in the same horizontal plane in which the needle moves by means of the counterpoise, and parallel to it, no declination is produced either to the east or west; but an *inclination* takes place, so that the pole, next which the negative electricity enters the wire, is *depressed* when the wire is situated on the *west* side, and *elevated* when situated on the *east* side.

If the uniting wire be placed perpendicularly to the plane of the magnetic meridian, whether above or below it, the needle remains at rest, unless it be very near the pole; in that case the pole is *elevated* when the entrance is from the *west* side of the wire, and *depressed,* when from the *east* side.

When the uniting wire is placed perpendicularly opposite to the pole of the magnetic needle, and the upper extremity of the wire receives the negative electricity, the pole is moved towards the east; but when the wire is opposite to a point between the pole and the middle of the needle, the pole is most towards the west. When the upper end of the wire receives positive electricity, the phenomena are reversed.

If the uniting wire is bent so as to form two legs parallel to each other, it repels or attracts the magnetic poles according to the different conditions of the case. Suppose the wire placed opposite to either pole of the needle, so that the plane of the parallel legs is perpendicular to the magnetic meridian, and let the eastern leg be united with the negative end, the western leg with the positive end of the battery: in that case the nearest pole will be repelled either to the east or west, according to the position of the plane of the legs. The eastmost leg being united with the positive, and the westmost with the negative side of the battery, the nearest pole will be attracted. When the plane of the legs is placed perpendicular to the place between the pole and the middle of the needle, the same effects recur, but reversed.

A brass needle, suspended like a magnetic needle, is not moved by the effect of the uniting wire. Likewise needles of glass and of gum lac remain unacted on.

We may now make a few observations towards explaining these phenomena.

The electric conflict acts only on the magnetic particles of matter. All non-magnetic bodies appear penetrable by the electric conflict, while magnetic bodies, or rather their magnetic particles, resist the passage of this conflict. Hence they can be moved by the impetus of the contending powers.

It is sufficiently evident from the preceding facts that the electric conflict is not confined to the conductor, but dispersed pretty widely in the circumjacent space.

From the preceding facts we may likewise collect that this conflict performs circles; for without this condition, it seems impossible that the one part of the uniting wire, when placed below the magnetic pole, should drive it towards the east, and when placed above it towards the west; for it is the nature of a circle that the motions in opposite parts should have an opposite direction. Besides, a motion in circles, joined with a progressive motion, according to the length of the conductor, ought to form a conchoidal or spiral line; but this, unless I am mistaken, contributes nothing to explain the phenomena hitherto observed.

All the effects on the north pole above-mentioned are easily understood by supposing that negative electricity moves in a spiral line bent towards the right, and propels the north pole, but does not act on the south pole. The effects on the south pole are explained in a similar manner, if we ascribe to positive electricity a contrary motion and power of acting on the south pole, but not upon the north. The agreement of this law with nature will be better seen by a repetition of the experiments than by a long explanation. The mode of judging of the experiments will be much facilitated if the course of the electricities in the uniting wire be pointed out by marks or figures.

I shall merely add to the above that I have demonstrated in a book published five years ago that heat and light consist of the conflict of the electricities. From the observations now stated, we may conclude that a circular motion likewise occurs in these effects. This I think will contribute very much to illustrate the phenomena to which the appellation of polarization of light has been given.

JOHN CHRISTIAN OERSTED.
Copenhagen. July 21, 1820.

Bibliography

Bibliography

In addition to general references in the history of electricity and magnetism, the following books and pamphlets are especially pertinent to the life and work of H. C. Oersted.

ALDINI, Jean, *Essai Théorique et Expérimental sur le Galvanisme*, Paris, 1804; 8°, 2 vols , plates

APPLEYARD, Rollo, *Pioneers of Electrical Communication*, London, 1930; Chap VI on Oersted; 34 pp , ports , plates

de BEAUMONT, Élie, *Éloge Historique de Jean-Christian Oersted*, Paris, 1863; 4°, 2, 48 pp Read at the session of the Académie des Sciences in memory of one of its eight foreign associates

Det Nordiske H C Oersted møde i København 1920, København, 1921; 4°, 152 pp , on the assembly of Norse scientists

FAHIE, J J , *A History of Electric Telegraph to the Year 1837*, London, 1884, 8°, 19, 542 pp , figs , plts

FIGUIER, Louis, *Les Marveilles de la Science*, Paris, c. 1870; Vol 1, cr. 4°, 6, 743 pp Replete with illustrations

GRAETZ, L , *Die Elektricitaet und ihre Anwendungen*, Stuttgart, 1895; 4°, 12, 511 pp , figs

HAMEL, Joseph J , *Historical Account of the Introduction of the Galvanic and Electro-Magnetic Telegraph into England*, London, 1859, 12°, 79, 16 pp Charles V Walker's copy

HARDING, M. C., *Hans Christian Oersted. En kort Levnedsskildring* København, 1920, 8°, 16 pp , ports

HOLST, Helge, *H. C Oersteds Opdagelse af Elektromagnetismen*, København, 1920, 8°, 16 pp On the discovery of electromagnetism

IZARN, Joseph, *Manuel du Galvanisme*, Paris, 1804; 8°, 4, 12, 304 pp., plates.

JOY, Charles A , *History of Electro-Magnetism and its Application to the Telegraph*, in Leslie's Monthly, Aug , 1878, pp 241-255

LAURITSEN, Laurits, *Hans Christian Oersted Et Blad af Fysikéns og Kemiens Historie*, København, 1909; Tl 8°, 135 pp , ports Biographical notes

BIBLIOGRAPHY

and a selection from Oersted's poems The Danish version of the
Experimenta is given

MEISEN, V, editor, *Prominent Danish Scientists,* Copenhagen, 1932, 4°, pp
89-93 on Oersted by Kirstine Meyer

MENDENHALL, T C, *A Century of Electricity,* London, 1887; pp. 67-110 on
Oersted and the Electro-Magnet

MEYER, Kirstine, See Oersted, *Scientific Papers*

MISSIRINI, Melchiorre, *Elogi di l'Uomini illustri italiani,* Forli, 1840; 4°, 50
biographies with portraits, including Romagnosi

MUNRO, John, *Pioneers of Electricity,* London, 1890, 8°, Oersted on pp
141-158, port

OERSTED, Dr (Hans Christian), *Om overensstemmelsen mellem de elektriske
Figurer og de organiske Former.* (København) , 1805, 12°, 22 pp , in the
Skand. Lit Selsk Skrift

Betragtninger over Chemiens Historie, en Forelaesning, in Det skan-
dinaviske Litteraturselskabs Skrifter, Kjoebenhavn, 1807, pp 1-54

Videnskaben om Naturens almindelige Love, Kjobenhavn, 1809; 8°,
30, 378 pp , 11 fold plates

Recherches sur l'Identité des Forces Chimiques et Électriques, transl
M de Serres, Paris, 1813, 8°, 6, 20, 260 pp

Experimenta Circa Effectum Conflictus Electrici in Acum Magneticam,
Hafniae, 21 July 1820, 4°, 4 pp. with certification of authenticity by the
Polytekniske Laereanstalt

Experimenta Circa Effectum Conflictus Electrici in Acum Magneticam,
in Journal fur Chemie und Physik, Nurnberg, 1820, pp 275-281 Followed by Neuere Electromagnetische Versuche, pp 364-369

*Experimenta Circa Effectum Conflictus Electrici in Acum Magneticam,
Expériences sur l'effet du conflict électrique sur l'aiguille aimantée,* in
Annales de Chimie et de Physique, Paris, 1820, Vol 14, pp 417-426

*Experimenta Circa Effectum Conflictus Electrici in Acum Magneticam, La
Découverte de l'Électromagnétisme faite en 1820 par J C Oersted,*
Copenhague, 1920; 4°, 46 pp. Preface by A Larsen; facsimiles of the
first Latin, French, Italian, German, English, and Danish announcements

*Experimenta Circa Effectum Conflictus Electrici in Acum Magneticam,
Zur Entdeckung des Electromagnetismus. Abhandlungen von Hans
Christian Oersted und Thomas Johann Seebeck (1820-1821),* Leipzig,
1895; 8°, 84 pp. Ostwald's Klassiker, No 63

Bibliography

"Meddelelse om Electromagnetismens Opdagelse," in the *Oversigt over det Kongelige Danske Videnskabernes Selskabs Forhandlinger*, May 1820-May 1821, pp 12-21 Contains the earliest account of the discovery of electromagnetism after the initial announcement of July 1820

"Thermo-Electricity,' in *The Edinburgh Encyclopaedia*, Edinburgh, 1830, ed , David Brewster; 4°, vol 18, pp 573-589, 2 plates

Ueber die Wesenseinheit des Erkenntnissvermoegens in dem ganzen Weltall, Kiel, 1846, 4°, 16 pp Read at the 24th Congress of German Scientists and Physicians in Kiel Inscr by Oersted to Bishop Martensen

Die Naturwissenschaft und die Geistesbildung, trans by K L Kannegiesser, Leipzig, 1850, 8°, 16, 170 pp

Aanden i Naturen, Kjobenhavn, 1850, 8°, 2 vols *The Soul in Nature* in the original Danish

The Soul in Nature, with Supplementary Contributions, London, 1852, trans L and J B Horner, 8°, 45, 465 pp , port Includes biography by P L Moeller

Der Geist in der Natur, Leipzig, 1854, 8°, 2 vols, port Transl by K L Kannegiesser, with biography by P L Moeller

Der Mechanische Theil der Naturlehre, Braunschweig, 1851, 8°, 21, 349 pp , figs

Kleinere Schriften, Leipzig, 1855, 8°, 2 vols in 1, transl by K L Kannegiesser On science, mythology and philosophy

Gesammelte Schriften, Leipzig, 1850-1, 8°, 4 vols in 1, port , plates

Gesammelte Schriften, Leipzig, c 1852, 4th ed , 8°, 2 vols , port

H C Oersted, Scientific Papers, Kirstine Meyer, editor, Copenhagen, 1920, 4°, 3 vols , ports , figs Collected works in the language of their publication with two essays by the editor, including a biography of 166 pages

Breve fra og til Hans Christian Oersted, edited by Mathilde Oersted, Kjobenhavn, 1870, 8°, 2 vols , port

Correspondence de H C Örsted avec divers Savants publiée par M C Harding, Copenhague, 1920; 4°, 2 vols , facsimiles

Ved Hans Christian Orsteds Jordefaerd den 18 de Marts 1850, 3 pp The funeral hymn

Hans Christian Oersteds Jordefaerd, Kjoebenhavn, 1851, sm 8°, 57 pp Eulogies following the death of Oersted

H C. Oersted's Slaegt (Copenhagen) , 1960, 8°, 8 pp. The genealogy of the family from 1582 to the present, prepared by H C Oersted III

Bibliography

sarton, George, *The Foundation of Electromagnetism*, (1820), ISIS, vol 34, June, 1928, 10 pp Portrait of Oersted by Bearentzen, facsimile of the *Experimenta*, etc, 1820 and the English translation in Thompson's *Annals of Philosophy*, 1820

schroeder, Jorgen, *H C Oersted, Discoverer of Electro-Magnetism*, Copenhagen, 1952, 15 pp, port, figs

smee, Alfred, *Elements of Electro-Metallurgy*, London, 1843, p 297 2nd ed, 8°, 30, 338 pp, illustr

stauffer, Robert C, *Persistent Errors Regarding Oersted's Discovery of Electromagnetism*, ISIS, Vol 44, Dec 1953, pp 307-310

Speculation and Experiment in the Background of Oersted's Discovery of Electromagnetism, ISIS, Vol 48, Mar 1953, pp 33-50 A new and informative contribution

taylor, William B, *An Historical Sketch of Henry's Contribution to the Electro-Magnetic Telegraph*, Washington, 1879, 103 pp A scholarly summary of early electromagnetism

thompson, Silvanus P, *The Electromagnet*, London, 1890, 4°, 4, 100 pp Inscr to Sir William Crookes

Index

INDEX

A Note about the Author

Bern Dibner is founder and director of the Burndy Library in the hitsory of science This institute was founded in 1936 to help provide sources of reference to the growing number of students in the history of science and technology. Some 14,000 books and pamphlets on the physical and biological sciences have been gathered in the Library The collection also contains manuscripts, portraits, and prints, prepared prior to 1900, intended to show the contributions from which the present scientific and industrial age has evolved.

Dr. Dibner is a graduate electrical engineer and holds a Doctor of Engineering degree from the Polytechnic Institute of Brooklyn. He is chairman of the Electrical Historical Foundation, a consultant to the Electrical Equipment Committee of the Smithsonian Institution, and has written several monographs in the history of science and technology